AUTHOR
KIT ELDREDGE

COVER/BOOK DESIGN
HELEN MULLINS

SLEEPWALKING

Going from one place to another without noticing your surroundings
(not unlike daydreaming)

SLEEPWALKING
Are You Living By Chance or By Choice?
© Copyright 2018, Kit Eldredge

ISBN 9781735562100

2nd Printing, 2020
1st printing, 2018

Kit Eldredge, author
www.bychanceorbychoice.com

Book/Cover Design:
Helen Mullins, HM Graphics LLC, hmgraphics@comcast.net

Printed at IngramSpark™ Publishing
Division of Ingram Content Group
1246 Heil Quaker Blvd. , LaVergne, TN. 37086
www.ingramspark.com

PRINTED IN U.S.A.

My Reason For Writing This Book

I dedicate this book to Marlene, my wife and life partner for over 45 years. Marlene is the woman that inspired me to have the courage, strength and confidence to believe and dream beyond my own imagination.

She also gave me our three children, Kristina, Michael and Catherine, who individually have lived a caring life that showcases their unique character, personality and choices.

Together they have helped me to discover the lasting version of the love my parents established throughout my childhood, with the help of eight brothers and sisters.

Thank you, Marlene, Kristina, Michael and Catherine for all your love, support and encouragement!

I'll love you always and forever.

INTRODUCTION

Hello my name is Kit Eldredge and I'm where I am today because, in so many cases, I didn't know any better... and I actually like it that way! In other words, I've chosen to live much of my life by chance.

I'm writing this book because it is about time.

Yes, the book is actually about time and being aware & in the moment but it is also about time that I converted "vapor to paper." (putting my thoughts in writing)

There is a common expression that goes: "If I only knew then what I know now" (sound familiar?) Well, I must say that I am excited about what the future holds because in so many ways, I know now, what I didn't know then. This book is full of expressions or sound bites that I've thought of throughout my life that serve as my "speed bumps" and cause me to slow down to ponder. Slowing down helps me to wake up from my sleepwalking & experience life more, better, longer as I continue to grow up.

However, as I've grown older, I've noticed how quickly time passes and I have recently discovered how to actually slow time down. I've begun to stop, look & notice more often and see people, places, things & situations in a way that I hadn't in the past. So now I'm writing this book to serve as my speed bumps, to slow me down or wake me up as I am sleepwalking.

If you've chosen to read this book, thank you.

PEOPLE ARE UNIQUE

I believe that every person has a purpose, a talent and a life experience that is so unique & special that no one else on this planet that has ever lived or is alive today is their equal. I'm a big believer in people and their ability to add value to the human experience by contributing to ideas that will make our lives better.

The sound bite expressions and thoughts within this book should sound familiar because they have all been said many times, in many ways, by many people throughout our history.

My hope is that the following sound bites will serve as your "easy to remember reminders" or "speed bumps" to slow you down or wake you up when you're sleepwalking, so that you can experience life more, better, longer as you too, continue to grow up.

MOMENTS LAST LONGER IF YOU NOTICE THEM

...See what's around you
...Listen to what's around you
...Feel what's around you
...Smell what's around you
...Notice the people around you

Now, that only took 10 seconds but you became more aware, you were more informed, you stopped sleepwalking for just a moment and lived your life by choice... Nice.

Looking forward,

We have more control over our Life than we think... Just not as much as we'd like.

-Kit Eldredge

(Easy to remember reminders)

SOUND BITES, PHRASES & EXPRESSIONS

THAT ENCOURAGE YOU TO

STOP

LOOK &

DISCOVER

4 > 2

THINGS HAPPEN FOR YOU, NOT TO YOU!

In other words, everything happens for a reason. There are no coincidences. You were born at precisely the right moment in time, in the right place, surrounded by the right people, taught/coached/inspired by the right person throughout your entire life and you are exactly where you are meant to be right now – as insane & wrong as that seems, at times.

In other words, we've all been "preparing" since birth for the moment we're about to go into.

WHICH IS THE GOOD NEWS!

Since we're all "perfectly prepared" for every moment ahead of us.

Want proof? Just take a moment to remember your past and then start CONNECTING THE DOTS (PEOPLE & EVENTS). **4>2** simply means that whatever happens in your life, good/bad, right/wrong, expected/unexpected, you can be confident it is happening FOR you and you have been PERFECTLY PREPARED to deal with it.

REMEMBER... things often don't make sense

at the time they happen but if you choose to slow down occasionally and stop, look & think, you'll begin to better understand who you are, so that you can better choose where you're headed.

BLUE PIECES

Let's imagine a puzzle for a moment

That puzzle is the planet earth. All the planet Earth puzzle pieces are shaped uniquely but there are many more solid blue ocean pieces than any other puzzle piece color. As our planet Earth puzzle is assembled, the blue ocean pieces may be the last area to place together because they look so much alike but eventually there will be a gap to fill with just the right blue piece. After being ignored for the longest time, blue puzzle pieces suddenly become very important, as everyone is looking for the right one to complete the missing section.

I believe people are like our Planet Earth puzzle pieces, so many may not stand out, yet every person has a place that they're meant to fit in. If we slow down occasionally and notice the people around us, we may discover where & how we fit in or we may help someone else find their place.

ACCEPT DON'T EXPECT

Accept people for who they are and don't expect them to be someone they're not.

"Are you kidding me?" Clearly this is where the expression, "easier said than done" originated. It seems to be human nature to put people into a category and begin creating expectations of them.

After many years of being surprised by people, in good & not-so-good ways, I try to resist building expectations too soon.

ACCEPT DON'T EXPECT

is a sound bite that reminds me to stop, look & consider taking a little more time to understand the person that was brought into my life.

Prejudging people or events too soon can lead to a lost opportunity.

OUR ANSWERS ARE ALL AROUND US, WITHIN THE PEOPLE THAT SURROUND US!

Consider this...

EASY TO REMEMBER REMINDER

and choose to

STOP, LOOK & DISCOVER

the resources around you occasionally. Notice the people you see, think about the people you don't see and remember the people from your past that you've learned a thing or two from. The answers are discovered when we start connecting the dots we've created throughout our life.

VAPOR
• • • •
PAPER
• • • •
PEOPLE

14

THINK IT
WRITE IT
DO IT

Creating something out of nothing starts with a vision,

or an idea.... VAPOR. If you believe in the vision,
then write it down so you can

begin a plan.... PAPER. Once your vision is
expressed on paper, share it

with other.... PEOPLE, that can help make it happen.

30 SECOND VACATI

This sound bite applies when you want to take a break from whatever you're thinking about but don't think you have a lot of time.

Simply begin counting to 30 taking one second between each number. As you count 1... 2... 3... 4... stay focused on only the next number and it will break your chain of thought that was on your mind.

While you're thinking about the next number, watch your other senses become more active as you notice things you didn't before.

During those 30 seconds of time, you may notice tree branches or grass blades blowing in the wind, at the same time you might feel a chill or warmth from the temperature, smell things in the air and hear birds and other sounds and then suddenly you reach number 30. Time seemed to slow down and you got a little break from your thoughts when you chose to stop, look and recover for a moment.

SUSTAINED FOCUS

This is a state-of-mind that may be difficult to achieve but often important to discover an answer you've been looking for.

It's basically choosing to be in the moment repeatedly to find an answer, solve a problem or enjoy a period in time.

A Day is a Lifetime

This expression is the result of being in the moment. When you're in the moment, time slows down. (See 30-second vacation.)

You'll discover there is so much that can be done in only 24-hours!

If you're feeling the stress of a deadline and your thoughts are spiralling towards a negative outcome, slow the day down by taking a 30-second vacation.

There are two thousand eight hundred and eighty (2,880) 30-second vacations you could take in a 24-hour day. Feel free to take as many as you want. You'll be surprised with how long a day can last and how much you can get done when you stop, look & notice the resources around you.

That first 30-second vacation may "prime the pump" for solutions and answers on how you will accomplish what you started thinking was impossible. In those 30 seconds, you'll break the chain of negative thought and be able to see, think and notice things you didn't while you were worrying about how much you need to do in such a short period of time.

Always remember, you've been perfectly prepared for whatever it is that you're worrying about! The answers, the knowledge & the people needed to help you, are all around you… you just need to stop-look & notice, once in a while.

Stop…Look…Notice!!

Look to
the Past
to see the
Future

Stop for a
moment and recall your
earliest memory. Then begin moving forward from that
point in your memory. This expression will help you

STOP, LOOK & CONSIDER

where you've been and have a better idea of where you're going. You'll begin to realize how people and events are connected and that maybe there were

NO COINCIDENCES.

Things may have happened for a reason, and you actually may be prepared for what lies ahead.

REMEMBER NOT TO FORGET

To understand this expression better, you'll want to close your eyes and remember a past moment in time when you felt happy or joyful. Enjoy that memory while you choose to do a **touch n' go*** in that past moment.

Was it that time you achieved your goal, earned an award, watched an event, were on a team

24

that won a game or championship or was it when you were amazed by something your child did?

Whenever your thinkin' is stinkin', this is another way to break the chain of thought, while you stop, look and remember the good times.

*touch 'n go means to only spend a few seconds on the memory and then go on.

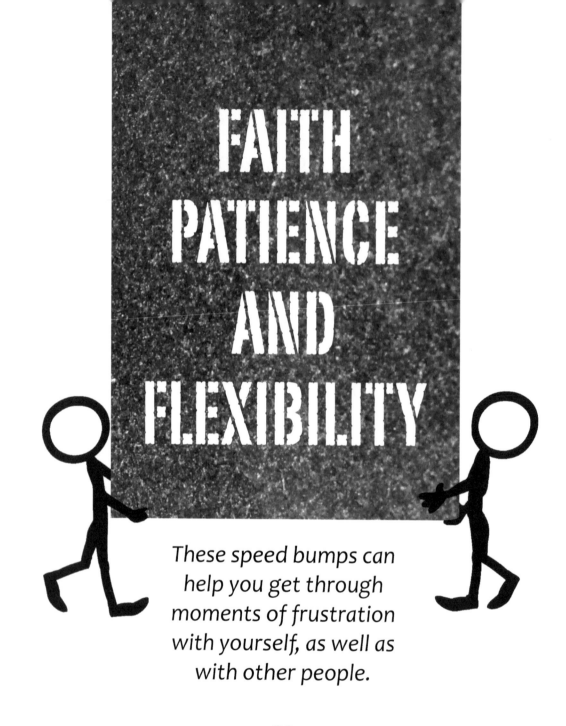

FAITH PATIENCE AND FLEXIBILITY

These speed bumps can help you get through moments of frustration with yourself, as well as with other people.

HAVE **FAITH** that things are happening for a reason (4>2).

HAVE **PATIENCE**, nothing happens as fast as we think it should. Try taking a 30 second vacation if you're losing patience to remind you that you have more time than it seems.

HAVE **FLEXIBILITY** in a fast-changing world so that you can adapt. As you practice FPF, you'll find it goes a long way to relieve some tension & frustration.

THINK IT DON'T SAY IT!!

This may be the most difficult thing to do but worth practicing!

It is the difference between "reacting" and "responding" to someone's comment or action.

The impact of your decision in that split second can be so dramatic that you could save or threaten a friendship, save or threaten a job or start or stop an argument with the one you love!

A RUT

A Random
Undeveloped
Thought

CAPTURING A THOUGHT IN THE MOMENT.

When you're in a discussion and you suddenly have an idea come to your mind that you think may benefit the discussion and you blurt it out so you don't forget it.

This is the opposite of "Think it don't say it."

RESPOND

DON'T REACT!

The difference between

RESPONDING and REACTING

to something that just happened can be

a split second.

Try to **THINK IT, DON'T SAY IT**

for 3 seconds and see if

that changes how you respond.

Remember, **10%** of our life is

determined by what happens

to us, but **90%** of our life is dominated

by how we respond.

BE AWARE AND ALERT

I'm reminded of this expression when something unexpected occurs in my life and I want to live by choice for a while.

When you choose to be in the moment you

become more aware & alert while you **STOP, LOOK & THINK**, observe or discover, which helps you make more informed choices when you could use them.

I Love
You
Dad

Who are you talking to?

I tell my kids, "I love you" and as they are turning away to leave, they will say, "love you, too." But they aren't even looking at me?

I simply ask them, "Who are you talking to?"

They stop for a second, roll their eyes as they turn back towards me and then they will say, "love you, too," while looking right at me...with a smirk on their face, of course.

I realize kids are programmed to repeat the phrase when they hear it from a loved one, but it's nice to be looking at each other when you say "I love you", so that the moment has a little more meaning.

Three stages of parenting.

The first ten or so years of a child's life is when parents get to Hold & Mold them.

This is the period when parents have a special bond with their child and can do no wrong. The child loves to be held a lot during the first few years of their life. This is also the period when parents will be able to mold their child's behavior as the child absorbs their parent's values, ethics and character over the first years of their life.

HOLD & MOLD

The teenage years are when parents could be Guardrails.

This is the stage of life when a child wants to explore on their own but could use Guardrails to keep them from wandering too far off course.

Once your child is on their own, the parent could act as a Safety Net for them.

This is the time when a parent can provide a soft landing when they fall, build them up when they're discouraged and be there to listen when they have questions.

SPELL NO

Know before
you say No!

Sometimes saying no is so final and might be the right answer but taking a 3 second pause before answering may lead you to discovering something that you didn't know or realize, which may cause you to be glad you didn't say no so quickly.

ARE YOU
SURVIVING

This is a question we all should ask ourselves from time to time.

Remember that everyone has a
PURPOSE,
TALENT & LIFE experience
that makes them so unique and
special that no one else on this planet
that has ever lived or is alive today is
their equal.

OR THRIVING?

Anyone that special
is capable of
thriving when
they choose to.

LOOKING FORWARD

This is an expression of receiving a planned moment such as getting together with friends, going to a movie, or any scheduled event.

However, if you're an uber-optimist like me, it also means you're

LOOKING FORWARD

to the

UNPLANNED EVENTS that may display the potential in people and life around the corner.

I also find it an appropriate way to sign off on letters & emails, rather than the usual; sincerely or regards.

Expect the Best and Deal with the Rest!

Be aware of the "best scenario" of anything you're about to do and ask..."Why shouldn't I expect it?"

You're perfectly prepared for anything. SO BE CONFIDENT that you'll be able to deal with anything less than the best anyway.

This may be why my brother tells me that you can never "pleasantly surprise" an optimist.

My wife, Marlene will tell me occasionally;

"KIT, YOU CAN'T DO IT ALL."

My response is always,

"SOMETIMES YOU CAN."

I've noticed that the more I focus on the moment, the less I focus on time, the slower time goes and the more I seem to get done. It doesn't make any logical sense as I write this but I have to go **with what I know** and what **I know** is that

$$4 > 2$$

I know that I expect the best and just deal with the rest.
I know that all my answers are around me within the people that surround me, if I am aware and alert and *I know* that as I look to my past to see the future, things may begin to make sense.

Yes, you can
do it all...
just not all
the time

I hope that since this book has found you, you'll find a couple of the easy to remember reminders that work for you and it will help you to slow time down and experience your life more, better, longer, with confidence that *you are always perfectly prepared* for whatever lies ahead.

Don't Settle

Shoot for the stars knowing
you may only land on

VENUS OR MARS

Enjoy Your
Moments
and Your
Memories!

About the Author

Hello, my name is Kit Eldredge and I was born in St Paul, MN and raised by my loving parents, Chick & Gerry, rounded out by a supporting cast of eight older brothers & sisters.

After graduating from High School and leaving home at 17, I thought I'd become a writer and photographer, until I met my soul mate and the love of my life, when visiting Seattle in 1973. Marlene & I settled down to raise three great kids and I went on to have a 40-year career in wireless technology, beginning with corporate life, then a couple start-ups of my own and transitioned to consulting towards the end.

But now *"I'm looking to the past to see the future"* and following my early dream of writing, with my first published book, which you've "chosen" to check out.

Thank you for reading my book!

Looking forward,

Kit

Visit: **www.bychanceorbychoice.com** to stay in touch.

CPSIA information can be obtained
at www.ICGtesting.com
Printed in the USA
BVHW020538151220
595404BV00004B/16